Toys & Games

ACROSS

1. This game has lots of pieces which you fit together to make a picture. (6)
6. In many board games, you have to roll these cubes with numbers on. (4)
7. This toy contains a doll on a spring that pops out when you lift the lid. Surprise! (4/2/3/3)
8. This cuddly soft toy looks like a woodland animal. (5/4)
10. This round item features in lots of outdoor games—you can kick it, throw it, or catch it. (4)

DOWN

2. It's got wheels and you can stand on it to ride along or perform tricks. (10)
3. You can put these wooden shapes together to create things. (8/6)
4. To play this, you must use a controller to guide the action on a TV or computer screen. (5/4)
5. You can play with this plastic bird at bath time. (6/4)
9. You hold this toy's string in your hand, and make it go up and down, up and down. (4)

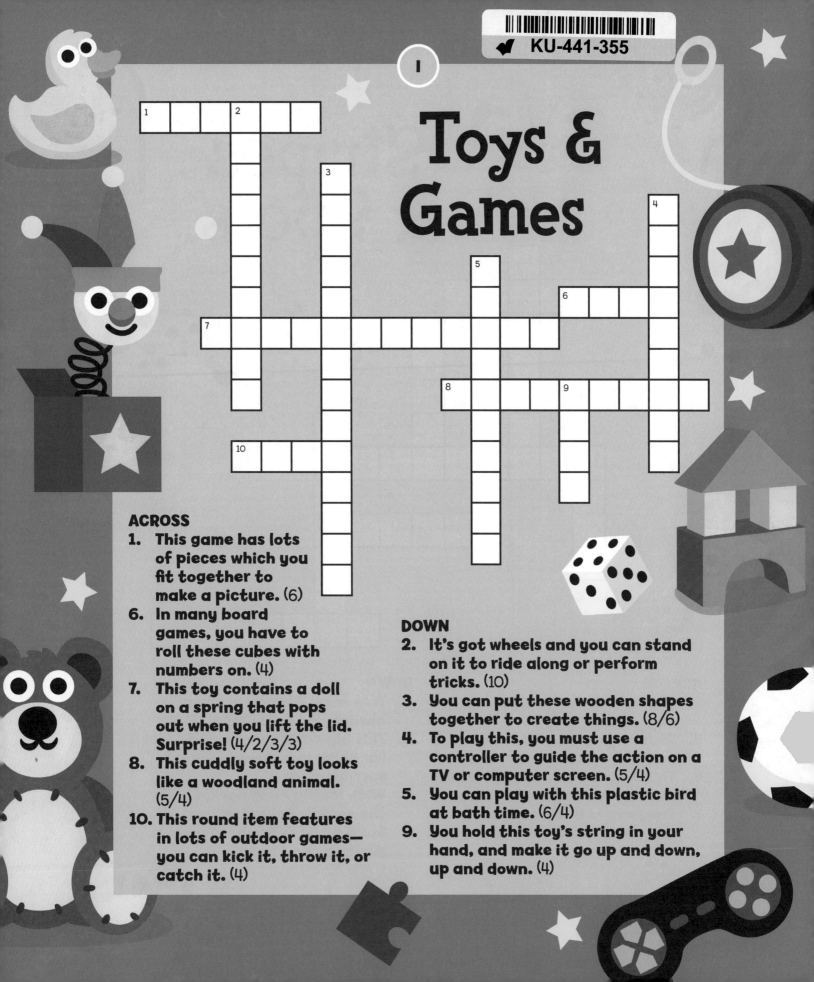

Stripes & Spots

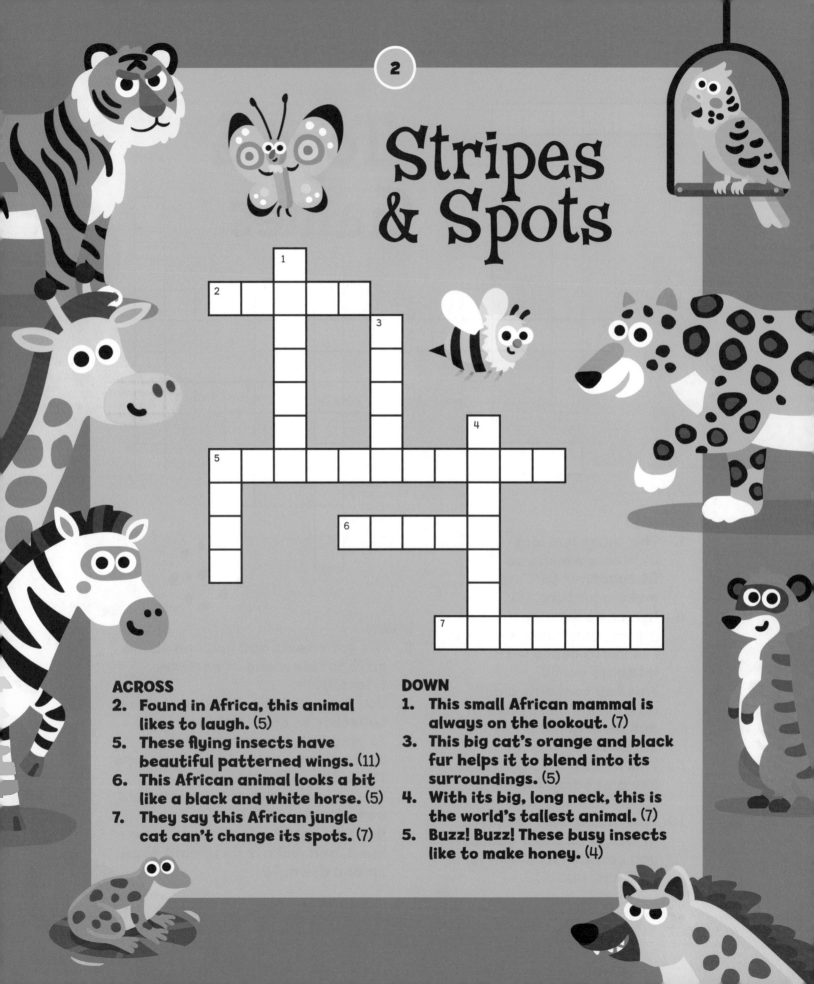

ACROSS
2. Found in Africa, this animal likes to laugh. (5)
5. These flying insects have beautiful patterned wings. (11)
6. This African animal looks a bit like a black and white horse. (5)
7. They say this African jungle cat can't change its spots. (7)

DOWN
1. This small African mammal is always on the lookout. (7)
3. This big cat's orange and black fur helps it to blend into its surroundings. (5)
4. With its big, long neck, this is the world's tallest animal. (7)
5. Buzz! Buzz! These busy insects like to make honey. (4)

WHIZZ KIDZ
Crosswords

Capella

This edition published in 2021 by Arcturus Publishing Limited
26/27 Bickels Yard, 151–153 Bermondsey Street,
London SE1 3HA

Written by: Joe Fullman
Designed by: Notion Design
Cover design by: Ms Mousepenny
Edited by: Joe Harris with Jessica Sinyor
Illustrated by: Matthew Scott

ISBN: 978-1-78950-309-8
CH007012NT
Supplier 33, Date 2210, Print run 10868

Printed in China

Things That Go

ACROSS

5. A set of automatic signals—red, amber, and green—for controlling vehicles at road junctions. (7/6)
7. This large vehicle travels on the road picking up and dropping off passengers. (3)
8. A big vehicle with caterpillar tracks that uses a mechanical arm to scoop things up. (6)

DOWN

1. A bicycle has two, a tricycle has three, and a car has four. (6)
2. This vehicle runs on tracks and stops at stations. (5)
3. The most common type of motor vehicle on the roads. (3)
4. A small two-wheeled motor vehicle. (7)
6. A large road vehicle used for moving heavy loads. (5)

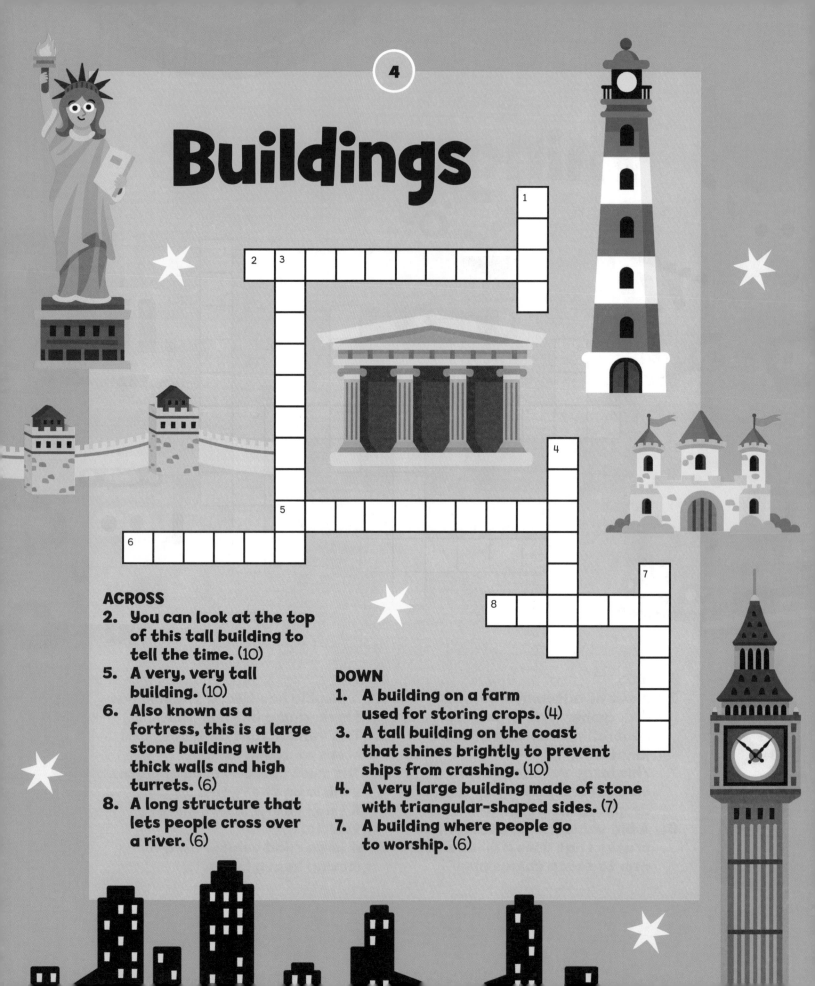

Buildings

ACROSS

2. You can look at the top of this tall building to tell the time. (10)
5. A very, very tall building. (10)
6. Also known as a fortress, this is a large stone building with thick walls and high turrets. (6)
8. A long structure that lets people cross over a river. (6)

DOWN

1. A building on a farm used for storing crops. (4)
3. A tall building on the coast that shines brightly to prevent ships from crashing. (10)
4. A very large building made of stone with triangular-shaped sides. (7)
7. A building where people go to worship. (6)

Sports Champions

ACROSS
3. What every winner is given. (4/5)
5. The official song of a country, which is played when an athlete is given their 3 across. (8/6)
7. What swimmers wear to help them see underwater. (7)

DOWN
1. Runners jump over these during a race. (7)
2. The fastest and most popular swimming stroke. (5/5)
3. A sport where people perform acrobatic feats on the balance beam, rings, and other pieces of equipment. (10)
4. A long pointed stick used in a throwing event. (7)
6. This flame is carried through several countries in a relay. (5)

Green Machines

ACROSS
1. She flies around on a broomstick, casting spells. (5)
3. This long, slippery reptile has venomous fangs. (5)
5. This green monster lives under a bridge and tries to gobble up anyone who passes over it. (5)
7. This giant reptile lies in wait at the water's edge, grabbing prey with its enormous snapping jaws. (9)

DOWN
2. This lizard hides from predators by changing its appearance to blend in with the background. (9)
4. This reptile lives in the sea. It has a shell and a powerful beak. (6)
6. This amphibian catches flies with its long tongue. (4)
7. This prickly desert plant is covered in spikes. Ouch! (6)

Countries of the World

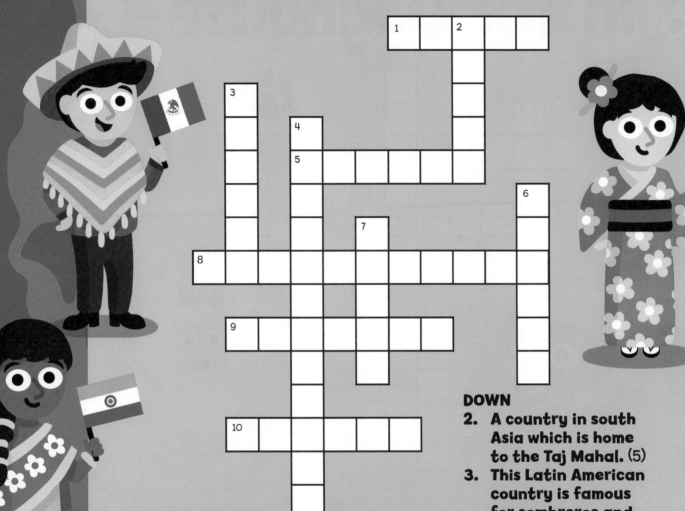

ACROSS
1. Giant pandas live in this country's bamboo forests. (5)
5. The largest country in the world. Its capital is Moscow. (6)
8. Nelson Mandela used to be the president of this African country. (5/6)
9. Berlin is the capital of this European country. (7)
10. Most of the Amazon Rain Forest is found in this country. (6)

DOWN
2. A country in south Asia which is home to the Taj Mahal. (5)
3. This Latin American country is famous for sombreros and spicy food. (6)
4. The queen of this country lives in Buckingham Palace. (5/7)
6. You'll find the Eiffel Tower in this country's capital. (6)
7. Cherry blossom trees cover this country each spring. Its capital is Tokyo. (5)

In the Doghouse

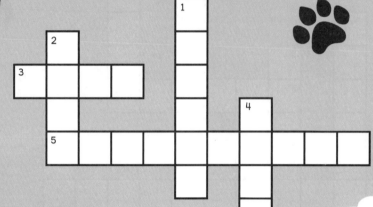

ACROSS
3. Dogs love to play throw and fetch with this. (4)
5. The daschund has a meaty nickname. Do you know what it is? (7/3)
7. A French breed of dog with fluffy hair. (6)
8. What you use to take a dog for a walk. (4)

DOWN
1. A band of cloth or leather fastened round a dog's neck. (6)
2. Some dogs have short ones. Others have long floppy ones. (4)
4. An outdoor house for a dog. (6)
6. Dogs love to chew and bury these. (5)

Fairy Tales

9

ACROSS

3. She waves her wand to make wishes come true. (5/9)
5. Snow White ate a poisoned one of these given to her by the evil queen. (5)
7. Jack climbed up one of these to reach the land of the giants. (9)
8. This sweet-tasting character escaped from the oven and can run very quickly. (11/3)
9. This enchanted rug can rise up into the air. (6/6)

DOWN

1. She had to leave the ball before midnight, but forgot one of her slippers. (10)
2. Rub a magic lamp and this character may appear. (5)
4. These characters made three houses: One of straw, one of sticks, and another of bricks. (5/6/4)
6. At 12 o'clock, 1 down's coach turns back into one of these. (7)
9. If you kiss this amphibian, he may turn into a prince. (4)

Winter Time

ACROSS

4. You might put one in your house and decorate it at Christmas. (4)
5. Something you do when you have a cold. Achoo! (6)
8. Christmas wouldn't be the same without him! He brings all the gifts. (5/5)
10. A yummy drink that's particularly nice on a cold day. (3/9)

DOWN

1. They keep your hands warm. (7)
2. You give and receive them at Christmas. (8)
3. He might have a carrot for a nose. (7)
6. Like roller blading on ice. (3/7)
7. Millions of these fall through the sky when it gets really cold. (10)
9. This keeps your neck warm. (5)

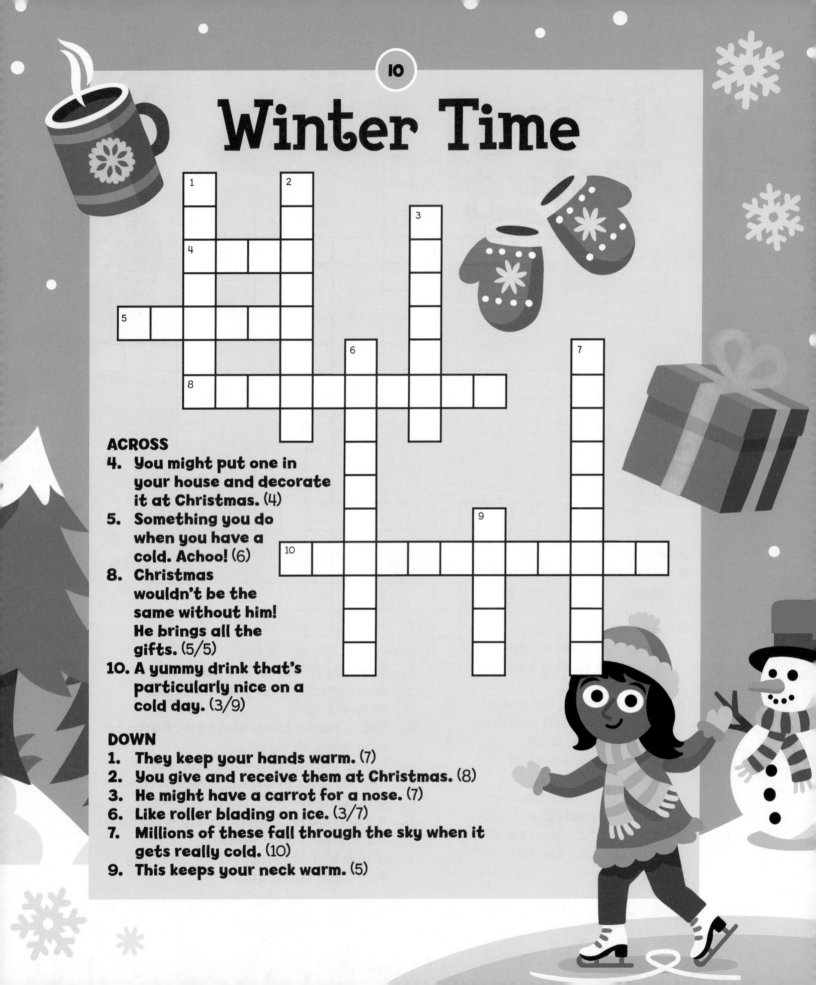

Artists

ACROSS
3. A stick of wax used for drawing pictures. (6)
5. It's long and thin with hairs on one end, and you use it to paint a picture. (5)
6. A wooden frame for holding a painting while it's painted. (5)
8. A small object that can be used to give 7 down a pointed end. (9)

DOWN
1. You can use this to draw a straight line, or measure how long something is. (5)
2. It's got two blades that press together to cut things. (8)
4. A thin board which artists put their paints on. (7)
7. You can use this long, thin object to draw pictures. (6)

Halloween

12

ACROSS

2. These spooky spirits look like floating sheets. (6)
4. People carve scary faces into these vegetables at Halloween. (8)
6. 5 down rides through the air on one of these. (10)
8. These Halloween monsters have long teeth and can turn into one of 7 down. (8)

DOWN

1. Old, dusty spiders' webs. (7)
3. What do you say to people who open the door on Halloween? (5/2/5)
5. She wears a pointy hat, casts spells, and has a black cat. (5)
7. These scary winged mammals only come out at night. (4)

At the Skate Park

ACROSS

2. You wear this on your head to keep safe at the skate park. (6)
3. A skateboard needs to have these round things to move. (6)
6. Some people like to skate while listening to music through these. (10)
8. Another word for "leaps." You'll see a lot of these being done at the skate park. (5)

DOWN

1. Shoes with wheels. Lots of people wear them at the skate park. (12)
4. A two-wheeled vehicle a bit like a bike, but without pedals. You move it by pushing one foot along the floor. (7)
5. You wear these on your legs to stop them getting injured if you fall. (8)
7. This bike can do lots of tricks. People like to ride them at skate parks. (3)

Predators

ACROSS
3. It has reddish fur, a big bushy tail, and looks a bit like a dog. (3)
5. You'll find this great white predator at the North Pole. (5/4)
6. The king of the jungle. (4)
7. This fearsome sea predator has a mouth full ofrazor-sharp teeth. (5)

DOWN
1. This eight-legged creature spins webs to catch flies. (6)
2. Watch out for this slippery customer or it might bite you with its venomous fangs. (5)
4. This silent hunter only comes out at night. Twit Twoo! (3)
5. This black cat prowls the forests of Africa, Asia, and South America. (7)

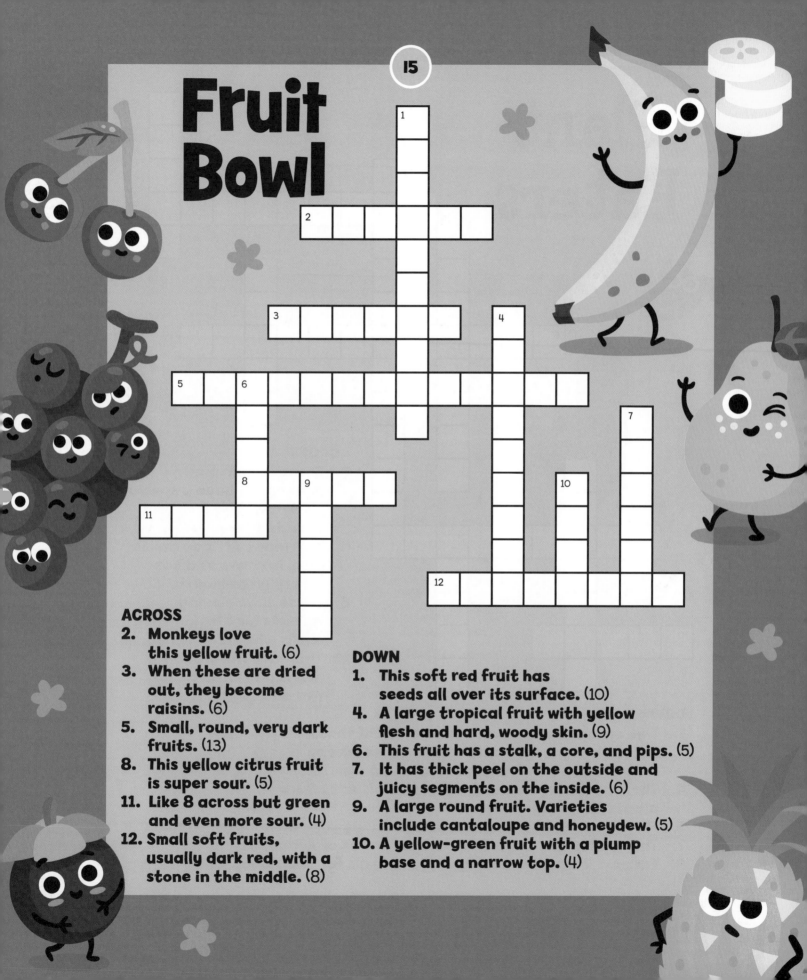

Fruit Bowl

ACROSS

2. Monkeys love this yellow fruit. (6)
3. When these are dried out, they become raisins. (6)
5. Small, round, very dark fruits. (13)
8. This yellow citrus fruit is super sour. (5)
11. Like 8 across but green and even more sour. (4)
12. Small soft fruits, usually dark red, with a stone in the middle. (8)

DOWN

1. This soft red fruit has seeds all over its surface. (10)
4. A large tropical fruit with yellow flesh and hard, woody skin. (9)
6. This fruit has a stalk, a core, and pips. (5)
7. It has thick peel on the outside and juicy segments on the inside. (6)
9. A large round fruit. Varieties include cantaloupe and honeydew. (5)
10. A yellow-green fruit with a plump base and a narrow top. (4)

Plant Eaters

ACROSS

3. These big jumping marsupials have a special pocket at the front for carrying their young. (9)
6. This giant African animal lives in rivers and has a very large mouth. (12)
8. These slow-moving animals hide inside their shells when frightened. (9)
10. This cute Australian marsupial looks a bit like a teddy bear. (5)

DOWN

1. This animal has a mane and four metal shoes. (5)
2. Before turning into butterflies, these creepy crawlies can be seen munching on leaves. (12)
4. The biggest land animal on Earth, this eats more plants than anyone else. (8)
5. This humped desert animal can go a long time without drinking. (5)
7. This gentle giant ape lives in the forests of Africa. (7)
9. Farmers keep these fluffy white animals for their wool. (5)

Under the Sea

ACROSS

3. People wear these on their feet to help them swim. (8)
5. A swimming reptile with a shell on its back. (6)
7. A vehicle that can travel underwater. (9)
8. A sea creature that walks sideways and has two pincers. (4)

DOWN

1. A gem found in clam shells. (5)
2. A small fish that sounds as if it should be ridden by a jockey. (8)
4. A soft-bodied animal with eight long tentacles. (7)
6. Someone who swims and explores underwater. (5)

Giant Monsters

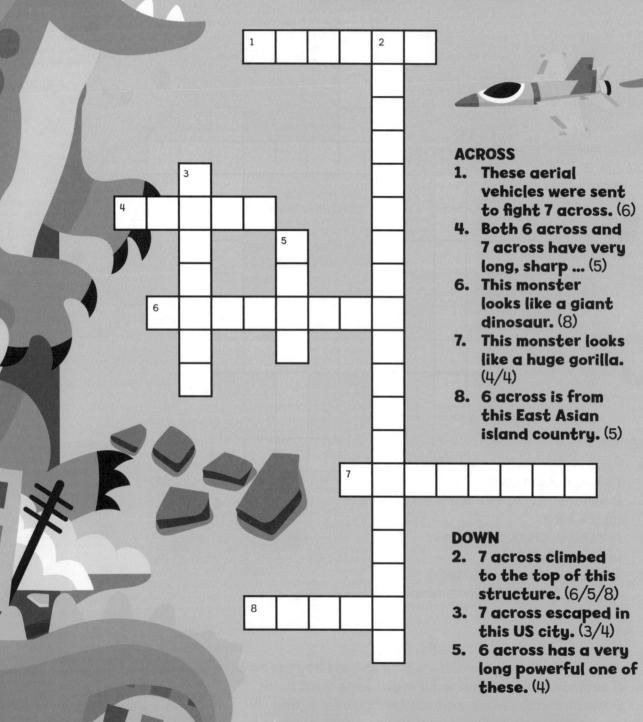

ACROSS

1. These aerial vehicles were sent to fight 7 across. (6)
4. Both 6 across and 7 across have very long, sharp ... (5)
6. This monster looks like a giant dinosaur. (8)
7. This monster looks like a huge gorilla. (4/4)
8. 6 across is from this East Asian island country. (5)

DOWN

2. 7 across climbed to the top of this structure. (6/5/8)
3. 7 across escaped in this US city. (3/4)
5. 6 across has a very long powerful one of these. (4)

Toolbox

ACROSS
2. A tool used for digging up the garden. (5)
4. Hold this device up to your eye to see things close up. (10/5)
6. Climb up this to reach high places. (6)
7. These strong pincers are good for bending and cutting wire. (6)

DOWN
1. This device has a needle that always points north. (7)
2. You can use this tool to cut things. It's got two blades which you press together using a handle. (8)
3. You can cut wood using this very sharp tool. (3)
5. This noisy tool makes holes in hard surfaces. (5)

Flying Vehicles

ACROSS
2. Flying vehicles that go very high have to go through these white fluffy things. (6)
6. This powerful vehicle can shoot all the way up into space. (6)
7. This vehicle flies using a fast-spinning rotor on its top. (10)
8. Old-fashioned planes are powered by these spinning blades. (10)

DOWN
1. An alien's vehicle—it looks a bit like a piece of crockery. (6/6)
3. You board this winged vehicle to go on vacation. (5)
4. To fly this, you need to lie in a harness beneath its wings. (4/6)
5. If you fill this vehicle with hot air, it will slowly rise into the air. (7)

Dancing

ACROSS

3. This word can be used to describe a dance, a style of music, and a place where you go to dance. (5)
6. You might wear a tutu if you were performing this dance. (6)
7. A dance from Spain featuring castanets and fans. (8)
8. You need to feel this if you want to dance well. (6)

DOWN

1. What you listen to when you're dancing. (5)
2. Someone who is bad at dancing is said to have these. (3/4/4)
4. You can dance on your own, or you can dance with a ... (7)
5. People in Hawaii wear grass skirts when performing this dance. (4)

Woodland Animals

ACROSS

2. A very large, brown animal with enormous antlers. (5)
6. An animal with long ears that hops around the woods. (6)
7. Ouch! This little animal has prickles instead of fur. (8)
8. A big, furry animal which hibernates every winter. (4)

DOWN

1. This red animal has a bushy tail. (3)
3. You'll see this cute critter bouncing around the woods in search of nuts. (8)
4. A slow, slimy creature which carries its home wherever it goes. (5)
5. A noisy bird with blue feathers. (4/3)

23

At the Seaside

DOWN

2. A flat, curved platform that people stand on to ride through the waves. (9)
3. A type of large white bird often found at the seaside. (7)
5. It's fun to build these mini fortresses on the beach using a bucket and spade. (4/7)
7. A type of loose rubber sandal often worn on the beach. (4/5)
8. Lick one of these to cool down—maybe have a cone! (3/5)

ACROSS

1. Women often wear these two-piece bathing costumes at the beach. (7)
4. It's common for men to wear these special shorts to go swimming. (6)
6. A round inflatable toy you play with at the beach. (5/4)
9. A tall building that shines brightly to guide ships to the coast. (10)
10. Wear these to keep the sun out of your eyes. (10)

Insects

ACROSS

4. This winged insect sounds like it should taste delicious! (9)
6. This flying insect sounds like it should be able to breathe fire. It lives near ponds. (9)
7. This insect sounds like it should be in church. (7/6)
9. These winged insects buzz around the house. (5)
10. These insects live in hives and make honey. (4)

DOWN

1. This long, many-legged creature will eventually turn into 4 across. (11)
2. This is made by 8 down to catch 9 across. (3)
3. These tiny creatures live in large colonies. Types include leaf-cutter, red, and army. (4)
5. 10 down need to visit a lot of these to make their honey. (7)
8. This creature has eight legs and many people find it scary. (6)

Instruments

ACROSS

2. The musician sits next to this large instrument, plucking the strings. (4)
4. You shake these in your hand to keep the beat. (7)
7. It has black and white keys and you play it with both hands. (5)
8. A long, straight woodwind instrument—you blow into a mouthpiece with a reed. (8)

DOWN

1. Beat out the rhythm on this percussion instrument. (4)
3. You blow into this curved metal instrument to make a sound. (9)
5. You can strum or pluck the six strings of this instrument. (6)
6. You use this to play a violin. (3)

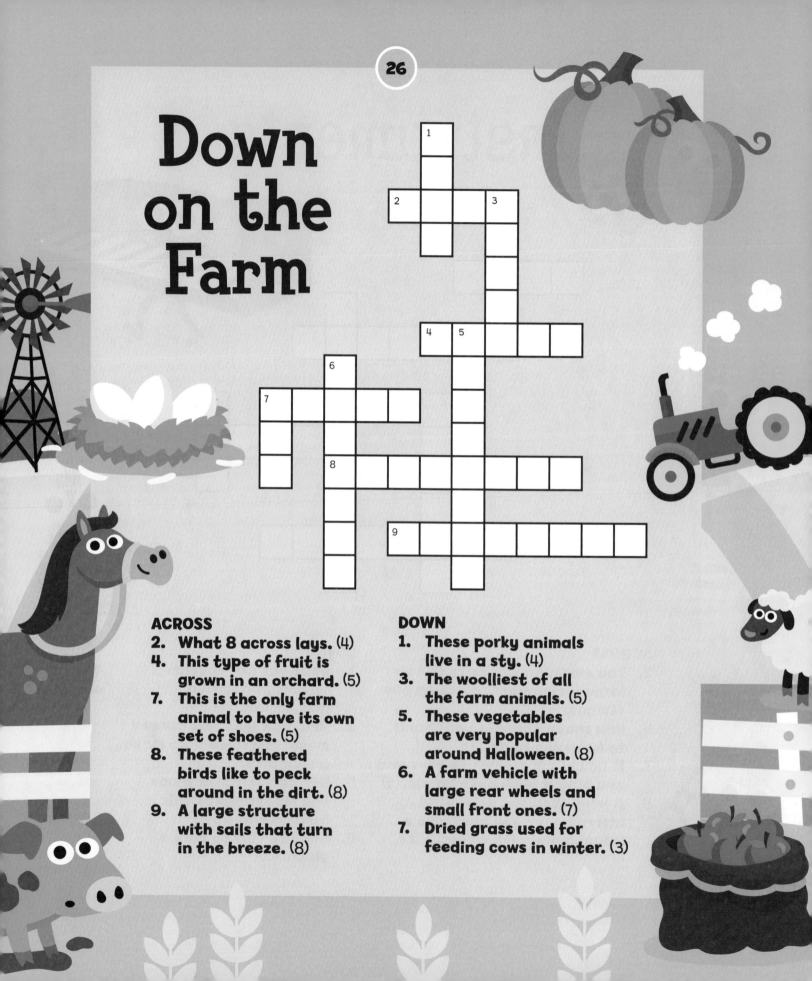

Down on the Farm

ACROSS
2. What 8 across lays. (4)
4. This type of fruit is grown in an orchard. (5)
7. This is the only farm animal to have its own set of shoes. (5)
8. These feathered birds like to peck around in the dirt. (8)
9. A large structure with sails that turn in the breeze. (8)

DOWN
1. These porky animals live in a sty. (4)
3. The woolliest of all the farm animals. (5)
5. These vegetables are very popular around Halloween. (8)
6. A farm vehicle with large rear wheels and small front ones. (7)
7. Dried grass used for feeding cows in winter. (3)

Solutions

1 Toys & Games

JIGSAW
SKATEBOARD
BUILDING BLOCKS
JACK IN THE BOX
RUBBER DUCK
DICE
VIDEO GAME
TEDDY BEAR
YOYO
BALL

2 Stripes & Spots

MEERKAT
HYENA
TIGER
BUTTERFLIES
GIRAFFE
BEES
ZEBRA
LEOPARD

3 Things That Go

CAR
TRAFFIC LIGHT
TRAIN
SCOOTER
WHEELS
TRUCK
BUS
DIGGER

4 Buildings

BARN
CLOCKTOWER
LIGHTHOUSE
SKYSCRAPER
PYRAMID
CASTLE
BRIDGE
TEMPLE

5 Sports Champions

HURDLES
GOLD MEDAL
GYMNASTICS
FRONT CRAWL
NATIONAL ANTHEM
JAVELIN
GOGGLES
TORCH

6 Green Machines

WITCH
CHAMELEON
SNAKE
TURTLE
TROLL
FROG
CROCODILE
CACTUS

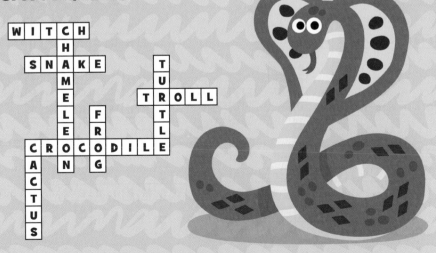

7 Countries of the World

CHINA · INDIA · MEXICO · GREAT BRITAIN · RUSSIA · FRANCE · JAPAN · SOUTH AFRICA · GERMANY · BRAZIL

10 Winter Time

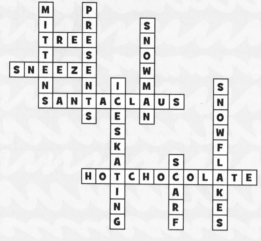

MITTENS · PRESENTS · TREE · SNEEZE · SANTA CLAUS · SNOWMAN · ICE SKATING · SNOWFLAKES · SCARF · HOT CHOCOLATE

13 At the Skate Park

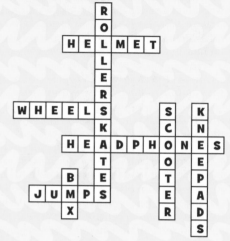

ROLLER SKATES · HELMET · WHEELS · HEADPHONES · SCOOTER · KNEEPADS · JUMPS · BMX

8 In the Doghouse

EAR · BALL · COLLAR · SAUSAGE DOG · KENNEL · BONES · POODLE · LEAD

11 Artists

RULE · SCISSORS · CRAYON · BRUSH · EASEL · PALETTE · SHARPENER · PENCIL

14 Predators

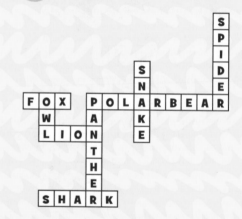

SPIDER · SNAKE · FOX · POLAR BEAR · OWL · LION · PANTHER · SHARK

9 Fairy Tales

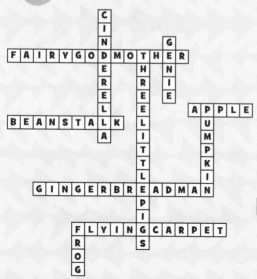

CINDERELLA · FAIRY GODMOTHER · GENIE · THREE LITTLE PIGS · BEANSTALK · APPLE · PUMPKIN · GINGERBREAD MAN · FLYING CARPET · FROG

12 Halloween

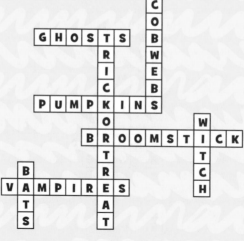

COBWEBS · GHOSTS · TRICK · PUMPKINS · BROOMSTICK · WITCH · TREAT · BATS · VAMPIRES

15 Fruit Bowl

STRAWBERRY · BANANA · GRAPES · PINEAPPLE · BLACKCURRANTS · ORANGE · LIME · LEMON · MELON · PEAR · CHERRIES · APPLE

16 Plant Eaters

HORSE

KANGAROOS
CATERPILLARS
ELEPHANT
CAMEL
HIPPOPOTAMUS
GORILLA
TORTOISES
SHEEP
KOALA

17 Under the Sea

PEARL
FLIPPERS
SEAHORSE
OCTOPUS
TURTLE
DIVE
SUBMARINE
CRAB

18 Giant Monsters

PLANES
EMPIRESTATEBUILDING
TEETH
NEWYORK
TAIL
GODZILLA
KINGKONG
JAPAN

19 Toolbox

COMPASS
SPADE
SCISSORS
MAGNIFYINGGLASS
SAW
LADDER
DRILL
PLIERS

20 Flying Vehicles

CLOUDS
FLYINGSAUCER
HANGGLIDER
BALLOON
PLANE
ROCKET
HELICOPTER
PROPELLERS

21 Dancing

Across / Down entries:
- MUSIC
- TWO LEFT FEET
- DISCO
- HULA
- BALLET
- PARTNER
- FLAMENCO
- RHYTHM

22 Woodland Animals

- FOX
- MOOSE
- SQUIRREL
- SNAIL
- BLUE JAY
- RABBIT
- HEDGEHOG
- BEAR

23 At the Seaside

- BIKINIS
- SURFBOARD
- TRUNKS
- SEAGULL
- BEACHBALL
- SANDCASTLE
- FLIP FLOPS
- LIGHTHOUSE
- SUNGLASSES
- ICE CREAM

24 Insects

- CATERPILLAR
- WE
- ANTS
- BUTTERFLY
- DRAGONFLY
- FLOWERS
- PRAYING MANTIS
- SPIDER
- FLIES
- BEES

25 Instruments

- DRUM
- HARP
- MARACAS
- SAXOPHONE
- GUITAR
- PIANO
- BOW
- CLARINET

26 Down on the Farm

- PIGS
- EGGS
- SHEEP
- APPLE
- PUMPKINS
- HAY
- HORSE
- TRACTOR
- CHICKENS
- WINDMILL